We are such stuff as dreams are made on;
and our little life is rounded with a sleep.

William Shakespeare (1564–1616), English playwright

"The Meaning of Life

according to the Great and the Good

Richard Kinnier, Jerry Kernes, Nancy Tribbensee and Tina Van Puymbroeck

PALAZZO

First published in Great Britain by
PALAZZO EDITIONS LTD
15 Gay Street
Bath, BA1 2PH
www.palazzoeditions.com

Design and layout copyright © 2006 Palazzo Editions Ltd

Art director: Bernard Higton

A CIP catalogue record for this book is available from the British Library
ISBN 0-9545103-7-2
Printed and bound in Singapore by Imago

Contents

Introduction

What is the meaning of life? That question has been asked millions of times for thousands of years. And it stubbornly will not go away. It is a question that most of us first ask as teenagers. It tends to resurface at the most reflective moments of our lives. Its contemplation is often preceded by tragic events or personal crises. Death is often nearby – usually the death of loved ones or the too-real contemplation of our own deaths. Our beliefs about or disbelief in God are inevitably central to the question. Because life is short, the question is somewhat urgent. Our response to it will determine the principles by which we live, as well as our goals and priorities in life. It will influence what, if anything, we are willing to fight or even die for.

What is the meaning of life? This book might not contain THE ANSWER, but it offers several hundred responses to the question. The main purpose of the book is to provide you, the reader, with some wise, stimulating, or at least interesting perspectives on why we are here. Such words of wisdom may help you in your own search for meaning.

The quotations and the chapter headings were derived from a study we conducted. The original article that describes the study is entitled, *What Eminent People Have Said About The Meaning of Life*. It was published in the *Journal of Humanistic Psychology* (Vol. 43, No. 1, Winter 2003). In that study we first conducted an extensive search for quotes on the meaning of life, consulting numerous books and articles in the process (see Acknowledgements, p. 223). We chose to include only quotes from "eminent" people, or those who are or were well-respected by their peers or the general population – not flashy or faddish "celebrities". Admittedly, even though we employed procedures designed to exclude superficial celebrities (consultation with experts in their respective fields and our own consensus), the selection inevitably is still subjective. Readers, of course, can make their own judgment on who they respect and read the quotes selectively. We chose the population of eminent people, not because they are most likely to have "the answers" but because they are widely respected and their ideas may have special merit. We believe that most people would be more interested in what Martin Luther King Jr said on the subject than what Jerry Springer or Paris Hilton had to say.

In the study we used a methodology known as content analysis to identify the major themes of the quotes. The themes we found became the chapter headings in this book. It should be noted that several people are quoted more than once under different themes – people often say different things about the meaning of life at different times in their lives. Thus, do not assume that one quote in this book represents everything the person had to say about the meaning of life. Take the example of the French Existentialist, Jean Paul Sartre. He is probably the most famous atheist of the twentieth century. His quotes in this book reflect his belief that life is meaningless and godless. Yet it has been alleged that on his deathbed he proclaimed his belief in God. King Solomon of the Bible is another example. During his search for what mattered most in life he considered wealth, power, and finally God. His search for meaning, like most people's search, evolved over a lifetime. It should also be noted that some of the quotes come from literature (e.g. one of Shakespeare's plays) or from lyrics in songs (e.g. Bob Dylan's *All Along the Watchtower*). We are not suggesting that a quote from a fictional character or a song reflects the author's belief. The point we want to emphasize is that readers should not draw any conclusions about any author's complete philosophy of life on the basis of any of these individual quotes.

The ten themes (and chapters of this book) probably cover all the major views that people have about the meaning of life. The quotes expand upon those themes. Some of the quotes may be cynical or depressing. Some are inspirational and uplifting. Most, if not all, are thought-provoking. That is the purpose of this book – to provoke thought in you. We invite you to search and reflect!

Richard Kinnier, Jerry Kerres, Nancy Tribbensee and Tina Van Puymbroeck

Chapter 1

" Life is to I

e enjoyed"

All animals, except man, know that the principle business of life is to enjoy it.

Samuel Butler (1835–1902), English writer and satirist

Carpe diem! Rejoice while you are alive;
enjoy the day; live life to the fullest;
make the most of what you have.
It is later than you think.

Horace (65–8 BC), Ancient Roman poet

It's a very short trip. While alive, live!

Malcolm Forbes (1919–90), US publisher

The true object of all human life is play.

G. K. Chesterton (1874–1936), English writer

Look, I don't want to wax philosophic, but I will say that if you're alive you've got to flap your arms and legs, you've got to jump around a lot, for life is the very opposite of death, and therefore you must at very least think noisy and colorfully, or you're not alive.

Mel Brooks (b. 1926), US humorist and director

Life is short, live it up.

Nikita Khrushchev (1894–1971), Soviet political leader

The whole life of man is but
a point of time; let us enjoy it,
therefore, while it lasts, and
not spend it to no purpose.

Plutarch (AD 46–119), Ancient Greek writer

Life is either a daring adventure
or nothing.

Helen Keller (1880–1968), US deaf and blind author and lecturer

We all live with the
objective of being happy;
our lives are all different
and yet the same.

Anne Frank (1929-45)
German writer and Holocaust victim

How do you measure success? To laugh often and much; to win the respect of intelligent people and the affection of children; to learn the appreciation of honest critics and endure the betrayal of false friends; to appreciate beauty.

Ralph Waldo Emerson (1803–82), US philosopher

The aim of life is life itself.

Johann Wolfgang von Goethe (1749–1832),
German playwright and novelist

I really feel sorry for people who divide their whole life up into "things that I like" and "things that I must do." You're only here for a short time, mate. Learn to like it.

Russell Crowe (b. 1964), Australian actor

LIFE FINDS ITS PURPOSE AND FULFILMENT IN THE EXPANSION OF HAPPINESS.

Maharishi Mahesh Yogi (b. 1917),
founder of Transcendental Meditation

*Be glad of life because it gives
you the chance to love
and to work and to play and
to look up at the stars.*

Henry Van Dyck (1852–1933), US poet

Dream as if you'll live forever.
Live as if you'll die today.

James Dean (1931-55), US actor

If you ask me for the briefest and more leisurely statement of my own answers, I would without hesitation name "The Dance of Life," slowly written during the most mature years of my life. I would add, as dealing with the same question – though in a way both more intimately personal and more fragmentary – the three Series of my "Impressions and Comments," now collected in one volume under the title of "Fountain of Life."

Havelock Ellis (1859–1939), English psychologist and writer

The nicest and shortest answer might be this:
We're here to feel the joy of life pulsing in us – now.

Joyce Carol Oates (b. 1938), US novelist

Find ecstasy in life; the mere sense of living
is joy enough.

Emily Dickinson (1830–86), US poet

*You try to make an interesting journey
between the cradle and grave. . .*

Robert Duvall (b. 1931), US actor and filmmaker

I think of life as some delightful journey that I shall
take when all my tasks are done.

Ella Wheeler Wilcox (1850–1919), US author and poet

We are here to be excited from youth to old age,
to have an insatiable curiosity about the world.

Norman Vincent Peale (1898–1993), US cleric and writer

*Life isn't a matter of milestones
but of moments.*

Rose Fitzgerald Kennedy (1890–1995), US Kennedy family matriarch

You might as well live.

Dorothy Parker (1893–1967), US writer and poet

I am so absorbed in the wonder of earth and
the life upon it that I cannot think of heaven
and the angels. I have enough for this life.

Pearl S. Buck (1892–1973), US novelist

Life is truly a ride. We're all strapped in and no one can stop it. When the doctor slaps your behind, he's ripping your ticket and away you go. As you make each passage from youth to adulthood to maturity, sometimes you put your arms up and scream, sometimes you just hang on to that bar in front of you. But the ride is the thing. I think that the most you can hope for at the end of life is that your hair's messed, you're out of breath, and you didn't throw up.

Jerry Seinfeld (b. 1954), US comedian and actor

Life is a boundless privilege, and when you pay for your ticket, and get into the car, you have no guess what good company you will find there.

Ralph Waldo Emerson (1803–82), US philosopher

Basketball is an expression of life,
a single, sometimes glittering thread,
that reflects the whole. Like life,
basketball is messy and unpredictable.
It has its way with you, no matter how
hard you try to control it. The trick is
to experience each moment with a
clear mind and open heart. When you
do that, the game – and life – will take
care of itself.

Phil Jackson (b. 1945), US basketball player and coach

My formula for living is quite simple. I get up in the morning and I go to bed at night. In between I occupy myself as best I can.

Cary Grant (1904–86), US actor

I see life as a dance. Does a dance
have to have a meaning?
You're dancing because you enjoy it.

Jackie Mason (b. 1931), US comedian

A wise man once said that all human activity is a form of play. And the highest form of play is the search for Truth, Beauty and Love. What more is needed? Should there be a "meaning" as well, that will be a bonus.

If we waste time looking for life's meaning, we may have no time to live – or to play. Our graceful, smiling cousins in the sea may be wiser than us.

"Consider the ant," said the Bible. Good advice, to primitive peoples struggling to survive in a hostile environment.

But perhaps we should consider the dolphin.

Arthur C. Clarke (b. 1917), English writer

Life is meant to be lived,
and curiosity must be kept alive.
One must never, for whatever reason,
turn his back on life.

Eleanor Roosevelt (1884–1962), US humanitarian

Life is the art of avoiding pain.

Thomas Jefferson (1743–1826), US president

If I go to a play I do not enjoy it less because I do not believe that it is divinely created and divinely conducted, that it will last forever instead of stopping at eleven, that many details of it will remain in my memory after a few months, or that it will have any particular moral effect upon me. And I enjoy life as I enjoy that play.

Sinclair Lewis (1885–1951), US novelist

I take a simple view of living. It is keep your eyes open and get on with it.

Laurence Olivier (1907–89), English actor and director

My happiness is not a means
to any end. It is the end.
It is its own goal.
It is its own purpose.

Ayn Rand (1905–82),
Russian-born US writer and philosopher

Mistakes are part of the dues one pays for a full life.

Sophia Loren (b. 1934), Italian actress

Life is not worth living unless one can be indiscreet to intimate friends.

Isaiah Berlin (1907–97), English philosopher and historian

Life itself is the proper binge.

Julia Child (1912–2004), US cook, author and television personality

I finally figured out the only reason to be alive is to enjoy it.

Rita Mae Brown (b. 1944), US writer and social activist

Dostoyevski is right when he says that the man
who is happy is fulfilling the purpose of existence.
Or again, we could say that the man is fulfilling
the purpose of existence who no longer needs
to have any purpose except to live.
That is to say, who is content.

Ludwig Wittgenstein (1889–1951), Austrian philosopher

*The question of the meaning of life is,
as the Buddha taught, not edifying.
One must immerse oneself in the river of life
and let the question drift away.*

Irvin Yalom (b. 1931), US psychiatrist

Chapter 2
66 We are here

o serve God**"**

I believe we are here to do God's will. God's general will is for us to join Him as mortal co-creators in seeking to apply means and ends that are consistent with His nature – which includes love, power and justice – in preserving and making the world, others, and ourselves all that it, they, and we should and can be.

Jesse Jackson (b. 1941), US civil-rights leader and politician

My treasure lies in battling against darkness and all forces of evil.

Mahatma Gandhi (1869–1948), Indian leader

We believe that we are in fact the image of our Creator. Our response must be to live up to that amazing potential – to give God glory by reflecting His beauty and His love. That is why we are here and that is the purpose of our lives. In that response we enter most fully into relationships with God, our fellow men and women, and we are in harmony with all creation.

Desmond Tutu (b. 1931), South African civil-rights leader

We must free ourselves to be filled by God.

Mother Theresa (1910–77), Albanian humanitarian

We are born to make manifest
the glory of God that is within us.
It is not just in some of us;
it is in everyone.

Nelson Mandela (b. 1918)
South African president

How would man exist if God did not need
him, and how would you exist? You need
God in order to be, and God needs you –
for that is the meaning of life.

Martin Buber (1878–1965), Austrian philosopher

Life at its best is a coherent triangle.
At one angle is the individual person.
At the other angle are other persons.
At the tiptop is the infinite person, God.
Without development of each part of the
triangle, no life can be complete.

Martin Luther King (1929–68), US civil-rights leader

I think everyone should do the best they can
and trust to the Superior Intelligence that rules
The Universe to attend to the hereafter.

Thomas Edison (1847–1931), US inventor

CREATION WAS NO ACCIDENT. GOD HAD AN INTENTION TO BREATHE LIFE INTO THE WORLD AND TO MAKE MAN HIS MASTERPIECE – SO IT IS WRITTEN IN THE BIBLE.

THERE IS NO QUESTION THAT EACH LIVING CREATURE POSSESSES A DIVINE SPARK OF GOD; ALL OF US, ANIMALS INCLUDED, ARE GOD'S CREATURES. GOD IS LIFE AND LIFE IS GOD. EVERY LIVING CREATURE, AS A CHILD OF GOD, IS OF THE HIGHEST IMPORTANCE, THEREFORE.

Isaac Bashevis Singer (1904–91), US novelist

God made us in His own image and he had some
purpose when He thus created us.

Marcus Garvey (1887–1940), Jamaican black nationalist leader

Life is possessed by everybody from the garden
worm up. It exists because the creator of this
universe wanted it to exist. He designed it so it
would perpetuate itself.

William Westmoreland (1914–2005), US military leader

All the wealth on this earth, all the wealth under the earth and all the wealth in the universe is like a mosquito's wing compared to the wealth we will receive in the hereafter. Life on earth is only a preparation for the eternal home, which is far more important than the short pleasures that seduce us here.

Muhammad Ali (b. 1942), US boxer

Fear God, and keep His commandments;
for this is the whole duty of man.

Solomon (d. *c.* 922 BC), Biblical king

*There is no happiness where there is no wisdom;
no wisdom but in submission to the gods.*

Sophocles (*c.* 496 BC–*c.* 406 BC), Greek dramatist

God asks no man if he will accept life. That is not the choice.
You must take it. The only choice is how.

Henry Ward Beecher (1813–87), US politician

Those of us who are Christians point to an event that staggers our imagination.
Christians affirm that God, the all-powerful Creator of the universe, became a man in
the person of Jesus Christ. He taught that God is love, and that He is willing to forgive
us when we commit our lives to Him. He offered us hope of an eternal heaven.
I believe that He is the answer to every individual's search for meaning.

Billy Graham (b. 1918), US evangelist

The purpose of life is to reach perfection. The rose starts as a seed or cutting, then grows and prospers with the sunshine and the rain. After a period of time the perfect rose blossoms. The human experience is much the same, except that the time span is much greater because man, before he can reach this state of perfection, must return again and again through many incarnations in order to conquer all disease, greed, jealousy, anger, hatred, and guilt… He must pattern himself after the masters of perfection, such as the great master Jesus. Wanting to be perfect is all that is required.

Willie Nelson (b. 1933), US singer

Our lives are merely strange
dark interludes in the electrical
display of God the Father!

Eugene O'Neill (1888–1953), US dramatist

Chapter 3

❝We are here
and self-actua

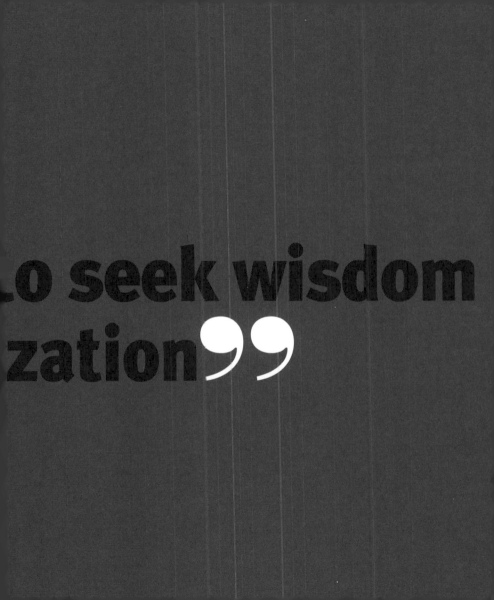

The question is not "Why are we here?" but "How should we live our lives?" The answer is to be found in Aristotle's *Ethics*. All of our technological advances have not changed that essentially difficult question.
The Greeks of the fifth century BC are our contemporaries; we are no wiser than they were. Remember Harry Truman's response when asked why he was reading Plutarch's *Lives*? Said the President: "To find out what's going on in Washington".

Mortimer Adler (1902–2001), US philosopher

THE LIFE WHICH IS UNEXAMINED IS NOT WORTH LIVING.

Plato (428 BC–347 BC),
Ancient Greek philosopher

Man's main task in life is to give birth to himself,
to become what he potentially is.

Erich Fromm (1900–80), German psychiatrist

*The aim of life is self-development. To realize one's nature
perfectly — that is what each of us is here for.*

Oscar Wilde (1854–1900), Irish writer

Life is a series of collisions with the future;
it is not the sum of what we have been,
but what we yearn to be.

José Ortega y Gasset (1883–1955), Spanish philosopher

To be what we are,
and to become what we
are capable of becoming,
is the only end of life.

**Robert Louis Stevenson (1850–94),
Scottish writer**

If a person sets out to achieve a difficult goal, from which all other goals logically follow, and if he or she invests all energy in developing skills to reach that goal, then actions and feelings will be in harmony, and the separate parts of life will fit together – and each activity will "make sense" in the present, as well as in view of the past and of the future. In such a way, it is possible to give meaning to one's entire life.

Mihaly Csikszentmihalyi (b. 1934),
US psychologist

The purpose of human life is to achieve our own spiritual evolution, to get rid of negativity, to establish harmony among our physical, emotional, intellectual, and spiritual quadrants, to learn to live in harmony within the family, community, nation, the whole world and all living things, treating all of mankind as brothers and sisters – thus making it finally possible to have peace on earth.

Elisabeth Kübler-Ross (1926–2004), US psychiatrist and writer

I teach you the Superman, Man is something that is to be surpassed.

Friedrich Nietzsche (1844–1900), German philosopher

We are all looking for a single purpose: to grow in wisdom and learn to love better.

**Rachel Naomi Remen (b. 1938),
US medical reformer and educator**

You cannot hope to build a better world without improving individually. To that end each of us must work for his own improvement.

Marie Curie (1867–1934), Polish scientist

Courage is the ladder on which all other virtues mount.

Clare Booth Luce (1902–87), US playwright and diplomat

Ancient religion and modern science agree: we are here to give praise. Or, to slightly tip the expression, to pay attention. Without us, the physicists who have embraced the anthropic principle tell, the universe would be unwitnessed, and in a sense, not there at all. It exists, incredibly, because of us. This formulation (knowing what we know of the universe's extent) is more incredible, to our sense of things, than the Old Testament situation of a God willing to suffer, coddle, instruct and even (in the Book of Job) to debate men, in order to realize the meager benefit of worship, of praise for His Creation. What we certainly have is our instinctive intellectual curiosity about the universe from the quasars down to the quarks, our delight and wonder at existence itself, and an occasional surge of sheer blind gratitude for being here.

John Updike (b. 1932), US author

I went to the woods because
I wished to live deliberately,
to front only the essential facts
of life, and see if I could not learn
what it had to teach,
and not, when I came to die,
to discover that I had not lived.

Henry David Thoreau (1817–62), US writer

The human species is in state of arrested evolution. We are not meant to remain in this primitive physical state any more than a tadpole is meant to remain a tadpole forever. Evolution is a one-way street: for example, when the first primeval aquatic beings moved up onto the land, they left behind their gills and developed air-breathing lungs. Today we can no more imagine the conditions of our future evolution than those fish could imagine life on dry land.

William Burroughs (1914–97), US author

Our purpose is to consciously, deliberately evolve towards a wiser, more liberated and luminous state of being; to return to Eden, make friends with the snake and set up our computers among the wild apple trees.

Tom Robbins (b. 1936), US novelist

Our minds are finite, and yet even in these circumstances of finitude we are surrounded by possibilities that are infinite, and the purpose of life is to grasp as much as we can out of that infinitude.

Alfred North Whitehead (1861–1947), English mathematician and philosopher

I learned... that no one can ever go back,
that one should not ever try to go back –
the essence of life is going forward.
Life is really a one-way street.

Agatha Christie (1890–1976), English novelist

The question of the value and
meaning of existence is unlike
any other question: Man does
not seem to become really serious
until he faces it.

Karl Jaspers (1883–1969), German psychiatrist

Chapter 4

" The mean
a mystery "

Life is an unanswered question, but let's still believe in
the dignity and importance of the question.

Tennessee Williams (1911–83), US playwright

I don't know whether this world has a meaning
that transcends it. But I know that I do not know that
meaning and that it is impossible for me to know.

Albert Camus (1913–60), French writer

Life is a fortress which neither you nor I know anything about.

Napoleon Bonaparte (1769–1821), French emperor

The most interesting thing in the world is another human being who wonders, suffers, and raises the questions that have bothered him to the last day of his life, knowing he will never get the answers.

Will Durant (1885–1981), US historian

Mere thinking cannot reveal to us the highest purpose.

Albert Einstein (1879–1955), German-born US physicist

There is an inexpressible confirmation of meaning... You do not know how to exhibit and define the meaning of life, you have no formula or picture for it, and yet it has more certitude for you than the perceptions of your senses.

Martin Buber (1878–1965), Austrian philosopher

Life does not consist
mainly, or even largely,
of facts and happenings.
It consists mainly of the
storm of thought that is
forever flowing through
one's head.

Mark Twain (1835–1910), US author

As leaves on the
trees, such is the
life of man.

**Homer (*c.* 900 BC–*c.* 850 BC),
Ancient Greek poet**

Now I have come to believe that the whole world is an enigma, a harmless enigma that is made terrible by our own mad attempt to interpret it as though it had an underlying truth.

Umberto Eco (b. 1932), Italian novelist

Scholars who have studied myth and religion for many years and have connected all of the theories spawned over the ages about life and consciousness and have taken away the superficial trappings, have come up with the same sensibility. They call it different things. They try to personify it and deal with it in different ways. But everybody seems to dress down the fact that life cannot be explained. The only reason for life is life. There is no why. We are. Life is beyond reason.

George Lucas (b. 1944), US film director

Why we are here is an impenetrable question.

Edward Albee (b. 1928), US playwright

What is human life? A vapor, a fog,
a dew, a blossom, a flower, a rose,
a blade of grass, a glass bubble, a tale told by
an idiot, a boule de savon, vanity of vanities,
an eternal succession of which would terrify
me almost as much as annihilation.

John Adams (1735–1826), US president

I miss the meaning of my own part in the play of life because I know not the parts that others play.

Rabindranath Tagore (1861–1941), Indian poet and playwright

Life is the art of being well-deceived; and in order that the deception may succeed it must be habitual and uninterrupted.

William Hazlitt (1778–1830), English writer and humanist

Life is the art of drawing sufficient conclusions from insufficient premises.

Samuel Butler (1835–1902), English writer and satirist

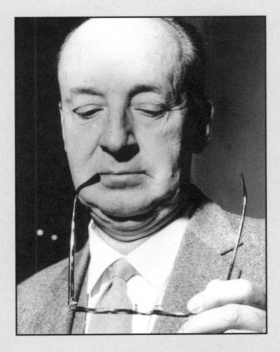

Life is a great surprise. I do not see why death should not be an even greater one.

Vladimir Nabokov (1899–1977), Russian writer

Life is what happens to you when you are busy making other plans.

John Lennon (1940–80), English musician

The very commonplaces of life are components of its eternal mystery.

Gertrude Atherton (1857–1948), US writer

I did not direct my life. I didn't design it. I never made decisions. Things always came up and made them for me. That's what life is.

B. F. Skinner (1904–90), US psychologist

I do not know what I may appear to the world; but to myself I seem to have been only like a boy playing on the seashore, and diverting myself in now and then finding a smoother pebble or a prettier shore than the ordinary, whilst the great ocean of truth lay all undiscovered before me.

Isaac Newton (1642–1727), English scientist

Life forms illogical patterns. It is haphazard and full of beauties which I try to catch as they fly by, for who knows whether any of them will ever return?

Margot Fonteyn (1919–91), English dancer

When I consider this carefully, I find not a single property which with certainty separates the waking state from the dream. How can you be certain that your whole life is not a dream?

René Descartes (1596–1650), French philosopher

Almost all aspects of life are engineered at the molecular level, and without understanding molecules, we can only have a very sketchy understanding of life itself.

Francis Crick (1916–2004), English scientist

Life in the temporal existence never becomes quite intelligible.

Soren Kierkegaard (1813–55), Danish philosopher

If we find the answer to that [why we and the
universe exist], it would be the ultimate triumph of human
reason – for then we would know the mind of God.

Stephen Hawking (b. 1942), English physicist

Life's meaning is a mystery. I'm not one given to theological musings, but I acknowledge these mysteries. In my own life, the profound root of my being – perhaps coming from my Jewish soul – is an existential imperative that we are here in order to carry forward the human condition, not just by having babies but by what we do with our lives. Whatever name we give to God, we sense that there is some purpose in ourselves and we are moved to purposes beyond ourselves. I celebrate my Jewish tradition; in my soul, The Lord, Our God, Is One.

Betty Friedan (1921–2006), US social reformer

The seeker comes in hope in finding something definite, something permanent, something unchanging upon which to depend. He is offered instead the reflection that life is just what it seems to be, a changing, ambiguous, ephemeral mixed bag. It may often be discouraging, but it is ultimately worth it, because that's all there is. The pilgrim-patient wants a definite way of living, and is shown that:

> The way that can be spoken of
> Is not the constant way;
> The name that can be named
> Is not the constant name.

Sheldon B. Kopp (1929–99), US psychologist

I wanted a perfect ending... Now I've learned, the hard way, that some poems don't rhyme, and some stories don't have a clear beginning, middle, and end. Life is about not knowing, having to change, taking the moment and making the best of it, without knowing what's going to happen next. Delicious ambiguity.

Gilda Radner (1946–89), US comedienne

On her deathbed –
"What is the answer?"
Alice is silent. "In that
case, what was the
question?"

Gertrude Stein (1874–1946), US writer

To find the point where hypothesis and fact meet; the delicate equilibrium between dreams and reality; the place where fantasy and earthly things are metamorphosed into a work of art; the hour when faith in the future becomes knowledge of the past; to lay down one's power for others in need; to shake off the old ordeal and get ready for the new; to question, knowing that never can the answer be found; to accept uncertainties quietly, even our incomplete knowledge of God: that is what man's journey is about, I think.

Lillian Smith (1897–1966), US writer and critic

Life is like Sanskrit read to a pony.

Lou Reed (b. 1942), US musician

Chapter 5

66Life is me

As for the meaning of life, I do not believe that it has any. I do not at all ask what it is, but I suspect that it has none and this is a source of great comfort to me. We make of it what we can and that is all there is about it. Those who seek for some cosmic all-embracing libretto or God are, believe me, pathetically mistaken.

Isaiah Berlin (1907–97), English philosopher and historian

The moment one inquires
about the sense of value
of life, one is sick, since
objectively neither of them
has any existence.

**Sigmund Freud (1856–1939),
Austrian psychiatrist**

All the world's a stage, and all the men and women merely players.

William Shakespeare (1564–1616), English playwright

It is a tale told by an idiot, full of sound and fury; signifying nothing.

William Shakespeare (1564–1616), English playwright

I am a temporary enclosure for a temporary purpose; that served, my skull and teeth, my idiosyncrasy and desire will disperse, I believe, like the timbers of a booth after a fair.

H. G. Wells (1866–1946), English writer

I do not believe in immortality, and have no desire for it. The belief in it issues from the puerile egos of inferior men. In its Christian form it is little more than a device for getting revenge upon those who are having a better time on this earth. What the meaning of human life may be I don't know: I incline to suspect that it has none.

H. L. Mencken (1880–1956), US journalist

What is life? An illusion, a shadow,
a story, and the greatest good is little
enough: for all life is a dream, and
dreams themselves are only dreams.

Pedro de la Barca (1600–81), Spanish playwright and poet

After thirty-nine years this is all I've done.

Dylan Thomas (1914–53), Welsh poet

Life and love are all a dream.

Robert Burns (1759–96), Scottish poet

We are here because one odd group of fishes had a peculiar fin anatomy that could transform into legs for terrestrial creatures; because comets struck the earth and wiped out dinosaurs, thereby giving mammals a chance not otherwise available (so thank your lucky stars in a literal sense); because the earth never froze entirely during an ice age; because a small and tenuous species, arising in Africa a quarter of a million years ago, has managed, so far, to survive by hook and by crook. We may yearn for a "higher" answer – but none exists. This explanation, though superficially troubling, if not terrifying, is ultimately liberating and exhilarating. We cannot read the meaning of life passively in the facts of nature. We must construct these answers ourselves – from our own wisdom and ethical sense. There is no other way.

Stephen Jay Gould (1941–2002), US paleontologist

Life has no meaning beyond this reality. But people keep searching for excuses. First there was reincarnation. Then refabrication. Now there's theories of life after amoebas, after death, between death, around death... People call it truth, religion; I call it insanity, the denial of death as the basic truth of life. "What is the meaning of life?" is a stupid question. Life just exists.

Jackie Mason (b. 1931), US comedian

There could be no other answer than what I was giving myself: What is the meaning of my life? – None. Or, what will come of my life? – Nothing. Or, why does everything which exists exist, and why do I exist? – Because it exists.

Leo Tolstoy (1828–1910), Russian novelist

Life has to be given a meaning because of the obvious fact that it has no meaning.

Henry Miller (1891–1980), US writer

Life, as we call it, is nothing but the edge
of the boundless ocean of existence where it
comes on soundings.

Oliver Wendell Holmes (1841–1935), US lawyer

[Life is] a blind, fortuitous concourse of atoms
not guided by an understanding agent.

John Locke (1632–1704), English philosopher

What makes life dreary is the want of a motive.

T. S. Eliot (1888–1965), US-born English poet and playwright

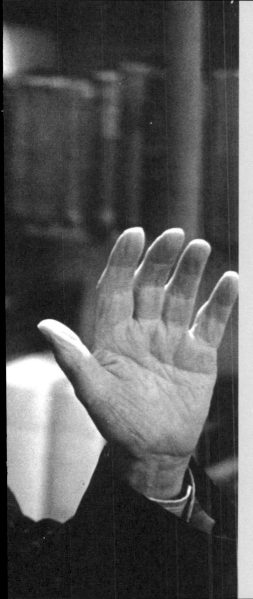

All the labours of the ages, all the devotion, all the inspiration, all the noon day brightness of human genius, are destined to extinction in the vast death of the solar system, and that the whole temple of man's achievement must inevitably be buried beneath the debris of a universe in ruins.

Bertrand Russell (1872–1970),
English philosopher and mathematician

I look on all sides and see only darkness everywhere.

Blaise Pascal (1623–62),
French mathematician

*We are so apt, in our engrossing egotism, to consider
all those accessories which are drawn around us by
prosperity, as pertaining and belonging to our own
persons, that the discovery of our own unimportance,
when left to our own proper resources, becomes
inexpressibly mortifying.*

Walter Scott (1771–1832), Scottish novelist

Life has no meaning except in terms
of responsibility.

Reinhold Niebuhr (1892–1971), US theologian

Life is a waste of wearisome hours.

Thomas Moore (1779–1852), Irish poet

If we must die, then our life has no meaning because
its problems receive no solution and because the very
meaning of the problems remains undetermined.

Jean-Paul Sartre (1905–80), French writer and philosopher

It's life isn't it? You plow ahead and make a hit.
And you plow on and someone passes you.
Then someone passes them. Time levels.

Katharine Hepburn (1907–2003), US actress

I am what I am. To look for "reasons" is besides the point.

Joan Didion (b. 1934), US writer

Nothing matters. [Last words]

Louis B. Mayer (1885–1957), US film producer

The greatest mortal consolation which we
derive from the transitioness of all things –
from right of saying, in every juncture,
"This, too, will pass away".

Nathaniel Hawthorne (1804–64), US author

Life is a short walk from the cradle to the grave.

Alice Childress (1920–94), US writer

The meaning of life is that it stops.

Franz Kafka (1883–1924), Czech author

The Oxford English Dictionary's first definition of "meaning" is: Purpose. Well, the more we discover about the real universe – not the fantasy one of most religions – the less evidence it shows of purpose.

**Arthur C. Clarke (b. 1917),
English writer**

Droll thing life is – that mysterious arrangement of merciless logic for a futile purpose.

**Joseph Conrad (1857–1924),
English novelist**

Has the question itself any meaning?

George Bernard Shaw (1856-1950), Irish playwright

No why. Just here.

John Cage (1912-1992), US composer

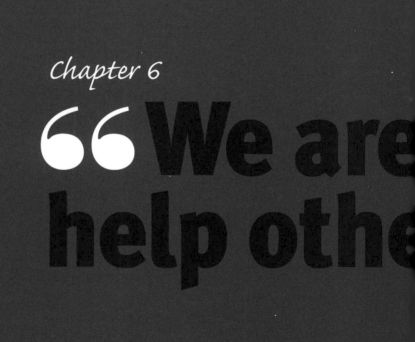

Chapter 6

**" We are
help othe**

here to
's"

THE LIFE OF A MAN
CONSISTS NOT IN
SEEING VISIONS AND
IN DREAMING DREAMS,
BUT IN ACTIVE
CHARITY AND IN
WILLING SERVICE.

**Henry Wadsworth Longfellow (1807–82),
US poet**

My consolation and my
happiness are to be found
in service of all that lives,
because the Divine essence
is the sum total of all life.

**Mahatma Gandhi (1869–1948),
Indian leader**

Service is the rent you pay for being.

Marian Wright Edelman (b. 1939), US civil-rights worker

Life is an adventure in forgiveness.

Norman Cousins (1915–90), US editor and author

What wisdom can you find that is greater than kindness?

Jean Jacques Rousseau (1712–78), Swiss philosopher

Three passions, simple but overwhelmingly strong, have governed my life: The longing for love, the search for knowledge, and unbearable pity for the suffering of mankind.

Bertrand Russell (1872–1970), English philosopher and mathematician

Only a life lived for others is a life worthwhile.

Albert Einstein (1879–1955), German-born US physicist

How strange is the lot of mortals! Each of us is here for a brief sojourn; for what purpose he knows not, though he senses it. But without deeper reflection one knows from daily life that one exists for other people.

Albert Einstein (1879–1955), German-born US physicist

The first thing I look at each morning is a picture of Albert Einstein I keep on the table right beside my bed. The personal inscription reads: **"A person first starts to live when he can live outside himself."** In other words, when he can have as much regard for his fellow man as he does for himself. I believe we are here to do good. It is the responsibility of every human being to aspire to do something worthwhile, to make this world a better place than the one he found it. Life is a gift, and if we agree to accept it, we must contribute in return. When we fail to contribute, we fail to adequately answer why we are here.

Armand Hammer (1898–1990), US industrialist

Why are we here? To take "Life 101," a curriculum of life experiences through which we can awaken into the fullness of our being. Such awakening involves learning how to acknowledge and contain within ourselves the polarities: separateness and unity, life and death, good and evil, activity and passivity, pleasure and pain, and suffering and joy.

Through this process we come to manifest, in our own unique manner, our heart's love and compassion for others, and our mind's clarity and equanimity and power. Thus is Spirit once again manifest truly in form.

Ram Dass (b. 1933), US guru

I BELIEVE IN ONE GOD AND NO
MORE, AND I HOPE FOR HAPPINESS
BEYOND THIS LIFE. I BELIEVE IN THE
EQUALITY OF MAN; AND I BELIEVE
THAT RELIGIOUS DUTIES CONSIST IN
DOING JUSTICE, LOVING MERCY, AND
ENDEAVOURING TO MAKE OUR
FELLOW CREATURES HAPPY.

Thomas Paine (1737–1809), English writer and revolutionary leader

I would like to believe that the highest state of evolution in our lifetime is to reach a state where grace and giving reign and we experience the oneness of ourselves with the creations of this universe. We must search for the good in each of God's creations; it is important to invest our faith in the best part of humanity.

Quincy Jones (b. 1933), US record producer and musician

There is a land of the living and a land of the dead and the bridge is love, the only survival, the only meaning.

Thornton Wilder (1897–1975), US playwright and novelist

A more abundant life is a more loving life, a life that loves God, Whom we don't see, as we love our neighbor whom we see all around us, all around the world. Love the Russians? Of course. Love that smelly, ragged old man sprawled on a subway grate for warmth? Certainly. Love the fellow with AIDS? Yes. Love the kid who just mugged you for drug money? Especially…
The meaning of life? There are these three: faith, hope and love, and the greatest of these is love.

Theodore Hesburgh (b. 1917), US Catholic theologian

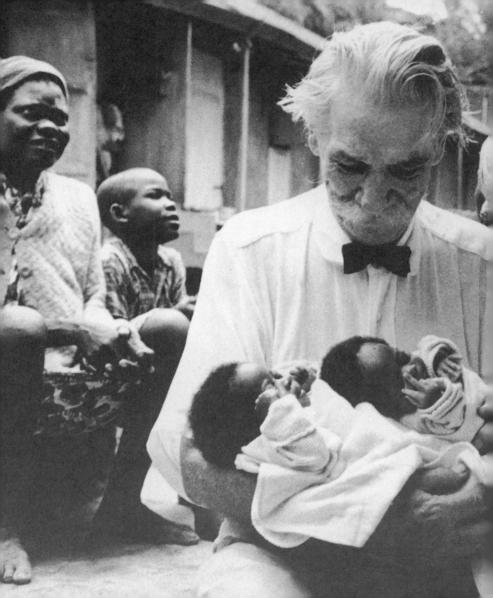

That everyone shall exert himself in the state of life in which he is placed, to practise true humanity toward his fellow men, on that depends the future of mankind.

Albert Schweitzer (1875–1965), French philosopher

Love alone is capable of uniting beings in such a way
as to complete and fulfil them; for it alone takes them
and joins them by what is deepest in themselves.

Pierre Teilhard de Chardin (1881–1955), French philosopher

Love is the ultimate and highest goal
to which man can aspire. The salvation of man
is through love and in love.

Viktor Frankl (1905–97), Austrian psychiatrist

The bread of life is love,
the salt of life is work,
the sweetness of life is poesy,
and the water of life is faith.

Anna Jameson (1794–1860), English writer

Each of us has a calling. *Voco*, "to call," is the Latin base of the word vocation. Thus each of us, not just clergy, is called by God to his or her vocation. No one on the giving or receiving end seems to regret this truth at the end of his or her life: that the key to life is service to others, service rendered in a way that is liberating and not demeaning. We are not each other's "keepers," we are each other's brothers and sisters. And it is in struggle and service with our brothers and sisters, individually and collectively, that we find the meaning of life.

Jesse Jackson (b. 1941), US civil-rights leader and politician

Life's most persistent and urgent question is,
"What are you doing for others?"

Martin Luther King Jr (1929–68), US civil-rights activist

But here we are. Not one of us asked to be here or had very much to do with his arrival. With our finite minds we cannot presume to know if there is a Purpose. We sense, however, the presence of something greater than we can comprehend, a force as yet unknown to us – perhaps ever to be unknown. So we accept our situation, learn from it, and do the best we can, resting on faith, despair or cynicism, depending on the individual. Overriding all this must be obligation – self-imposed or externally impressed – to do the best one can for others, to relieve suffering and to exercise compassion. We are all in this together, for life is a common, not an individual endeavor.

Harry Blackmun (1908–99), US Supreme Court Justice

Be kind and helpful toward our friends and fellow passengers who are clinging to the same speck of dirt while we are drifting side by side to our common doom.

Clarence Darrow (1857–1938), US lawyer

We are here to learn to live. Learning to love is terribly demanding and horribly discouraging. Some people never get anywhere with it. And no one ever gets a Ph.D. in the subject... The most concentrated lesson I have ever learned came to me as I stroked my wife's sweaty hands during her arduous birthing of our son, Nicholas. That single afternoon in a tiled delivery room taught me more about why we are here than did years of lectures and seminars. The world is designed to teach us to love.

Harvey Cox (b. 1929), US theology professor and writer

I believe that the rendering of useful service is the common duty of mankind and that only in the purifying fire of sacrifice is the dross of selfishness consumed and the greatness of the human soul set free.

John D. Rockefeller (1839–1937), US industrialist and philanthropist

When there is a hole someplace in the world, I believe a warmth eventually fills it. When there is poverty, a richness of spirit eventually comes to help. I believe we are here for each other; to lift, to encourage, to dream. Without that kind of giving we cease to exist.

Marlee Matlin (b. 1965), US actress

It is possible that on a spiritual level we are all connected in a way that continues beyond the comings and goings of various life forms…

If we have a meaningful place in this process, it is to try and fit into a healthy, symbiotic relationship with other life forms. Everybody, ultimately, is trying to reach a harmony with the other parts of the life force. And in trying to figure out what life is all about, we ultimately come down to expressions of compassion and love, helping the rest of the life force, caring about others without any conditions or expectations, without expecting to get anything in return. This is expressed in every religion, by every prophet.

George Lucas (b. 1944), US film director

I believe mass communication has helped make us all closer today than we've ever been. And I believe that the gathering and dissemination of worthwhile information to all the peoples of the world is the most important tool we have for achieving the end of realizing that our planet is the address for paradise.

Ted Turner (b. 1938), US media mogul

We are here to be vigilant, to be aware of the terrible things we can prevent – like the Holocaust, like Hiroshima, like hunger and want. There is a Jewish lullaby that says that we are like a river's shores, and deep, deep in us runs what has been, what we are now and what is to be transmitted in the next generation.

Ruth Westheimer (b. 1928), German-born US television personality

Chapter 7

"Life is a

struggle"

Life is one long struggle in the dark.

Lucretius (*c.* 96 BC–*c.* 55 BC), Ancient Roman philosopher

*Any idiot can face a crisis – it's
day to day living that wears you out.*

Anton Chekhov (1860–1904), Russian playwright

Life is suffering.

Gautama Siddharta (563–483 BC), Hindu prince and founder of Buddhism

Life is one damned horrid grind.

Charles Dickens (1812-1870), English writer.

Youth is a blunder;

manhood a struggle;

old age a regret.

Benjamin Disraeli (1804–81), English prime minister

Life is a gamble at terrible odds.
If it were a bet, you would not take it.

Tom Stoppard (b. 1937), English playwright

Life – the way it really is – is a battle
not between Good and Bad, but between
Bad and Worse.

Joseph Brodsky (1940–96), Russian-born US poet

You fall out of your mother's womb,
you crawl across open country under fire,
and drop into your grave.

Quentin Crisp (1908–99), English writer

As for life, it is a battle and a sojourning in a strange land; but the fame that comes after is oblivion.

Marcus Aurelius Antoninus (AD 188–217), Ancient Roman emperor

Life is a predicament which precedes death.

Henry James (1843–1916), US-born English writer

It is not true that life is one damn thing after another. It is the same damn thing over and over again.

Edna St Vincent Millay (1892–1950), US poet

Life is a tragedy wherein we sit as spectators for a while and then act our part in it.

Jonathan Swift (1667–1745), English author

Life is not a spectacle or a feast, it is a predicament.

George Santayana (1863–1952), US philosopher and writer

Life is a tragedy when seen in close-up but a comedy in long-shot.

Charlie Chaplin (1889–1977), English actor

There are some laughs you have in life, provided by comedians and provided by fortuitous moments with your family or friends or something. But most of it is tragic. You're born and you don't know why. You're here, you don't know why. You go, you die. People suffer. People live in constant terror. The world is full of poverty and corruption and war and Nazis and tsunamis... The net result, the final count is, you lose, you don't beat the house.

Woody Allen (b. 1935), US film director and actor

Life is work, and everything you do is so much more experience.

Henry Ford (1863–1947),
US businessman

You do not know what life means when all
the difficulties are removed.

Jane Addams (1860–1935), US pioneer social worker

We were born to struggle, to face the challenges
of our lifetime and, ultimately, to evolve to a
higher consciousness.

Quincy Jones (b. 1933), US record producer and musician

There is suffering in life, and there are defeats. No one can avoid them. But it's better to lose some of the battles in the struggles for your dreams than to be defeated without ever knowing what you're fighting for.

Paulo Coelho (b. 1947), Brazilian novelist

A man does what he must, in spite of personal consequences, in spite of obstacles and dangers and pressures. And this is the basis of all human morality.

John F. Kennedy (1917–63), US president

Life is a long lesson in humility.

J. M. Barrie (1860–1937), Scottish writer

My aim in life has always been to hold my own with whatever's going. Not against: with.

Robert Frost (1874–1963), US poet

[Life is] only a constant struggle for mere existence, with the certainty of losing it at long last.

Arthur Schopenhauer (1788–1860), German philosopher

Life should be
considered an art;
and we should create
the circumstances,
with which to
overcome difficulty.

John Dewey (1859–1952), US philosopher

It's gonna be a long hard drag, but we'll make it.

Janis Joplin (1943–70), US singer

Life is not an easy matter...
You cannot live through it without
falling into frustration and
cynicism unless you have before
you a great idea which raises you
above personal misery, above
weakness, above all kinds of
perfidy and baseness.

**Leon Trotsky (1879–1940),
Russian political leader**

Chapter 8

"We are her to society"

to contribute

We make a living by what we get,
but we make a life by what we give.

Winston Churchill (1874–1965), British prime minister

Be ashamed to die until you have won
some victory for humanity.

Horace Mann (1796–1859), US educator

*You must be the change you wish
to see in the world.*

Mahatma Gandhi (1869–1948), Indian leader

Life does not consist in thinking,
it consists in acting.

Woodrow Wilson (1856–1924), US president

If you have not found something to die for, you have no reason to live.

Malcolm X (1925–65), US civil-rights activist

To this day I believe we are here on earth to live, to grow up and do what we can to make this world a better place for all people to enjoy freedom. Differences of race, nationality or religion should not be used to deny any human being citizenship rights or privileges. Life is to be lived to its fullest so that death is just another chapter. Memories of our lives, our works and our deeds will continue in others.

Rosa Parks (1913–2005), US civil-rights activist

I can only tell you that I have found mental equilibrium and strength and inspiration in the thought that I am doing my bit for a mighty cause and that my labour cannot be in vain. I work for results of course. I want to go rapidly towards my objective. But fundamentally even the results of action do not worry me so much. Action itself, so long as I am convinced that it is right action, gives me satisfaction.

Jawaharlal Nehru (1889–1964), Indian prime minister

I had what might be truly called an object
in life; to be a reformer of the world.

John Stuart Mill (1806–73), English philosopher

*We are here to add what we can to life,
not to get what we can from life.*

William Osler (1849–1919), Canadian physician

Only a life lived for others is worth living. We cannot live a full life unless we have a purpose bigger than ourselves.

Richard Nixon (1913–94), US president

The meaning of life lies in the chance it gives us to produce, or contribute to something greater than ourselves. It need not be a family (although that is the direct and broadest road which nature in her blind wisdom has provided for even the simplest soul); it can be any group that can call out all the latent nobility of the individual, and give him a cause to work for that shall not be shattered by his death.

Will Durant (1885–1981), US historian

Each of us has a responsibility for being alive:
one responsibility to creation, of which we are a part,
another to the creator – a debt we repay by trying
to extend our areas of comprehension.

Maya Angelou (b. 1928), US writer

I was brought up to believe that the only
thing worth doing was to add to the sum of
accurate information in the world.

Margaret Mead (1901–78), US anthropologist

While we exist as human beings, we are like tourists on holiday. If we play havoc and cause disturbance, our visit is meaningless. If during our short stay – 100 years at most – we live peacefully, help others and, at the very least, refrain from harming or upsetting them, our visit is worthwhile. What is important is to see how we can best lead a meaningful everyday life, how we can bring about peace and harmony in our minds, how we can help contribute to society.

The Dalai Lama (b. 1935), Tibetan religious leader

If you would not be forgotten, as soon as you are dead and rotten, either write worth reading, or do things worth the writing.

Benjamin Franklin (1706–90), US statesman and writer

The great end of life is not knowledge, but action.

Thomas Huxley (1825–95), English biologist

Really the writer doesn't want success... He knows he has
a short span of life, that day will come when he must pass
through the wall of oblivion, and he wants to leave a
scratch on the wall – Kilroy was here – that somebody a
hundred, or a thousand years later will see.

William Faulkner (1897–1962), US writer

The true joy of life is being used for a purpose recognized by yourself as a mighty one ... being thoroughly worn out before you are thrown to the scrap heap ... being a force of nature instead of a feverish, selfish clot of ailments and grievances.

George Bernard Shaw (1856–1950), Irish playwright

Although only a small fraction of those who try to scale the heights of human achievement arrive anywhere close to the summit, it is imperative that there be a multitude of climbers. Otherwise the summit may not be reached by anybody. The individually lost and forgotten multitudes have not lived in vain, provided that they, too, made the efforts to climb.

Pierre Teilhard de Chardin (1881–1955), French philosopher

We are here as a result of random occurrences. But what we accomplish since we are here may give some sense of meaning to our existence. Although the notion of "here" can be simply defined as the brief physical time that we exist as individuals, we have the ability to make that "here" extend beyond this physical existence. Man is part of a "collective consciousness." We are connected to one another through time by our creations, works, images, thoughts and writings.
We communicate to future generations what we are, what we have been, hopefully influencing for the better what we will become. Our lives are given meaning by our actions – accomplishments made while we are "here" that extend beyond our own time.

Maya Lin (b. 1959), US architect

To make a dent.

Studs Terkel (b. 1912), US writer

Chapter 9

66**We must c
for ourselves**

eate meaning

"

What matters ... is not the meaning of life in general but rather the specific meaning of a person's life at a given moment. To put the question in general terms would be comparable to the question posed to a chess champion: "Tell me, Master, what is the best move in the world?"

Viktor Frankl (1905–97), Austrian psychiatrist

Believe that life is worth living and your belief will help create the fact.

William James (1842–1910), US philosopher

Man is indispensable for the completion of creation; that is, in fact, he himself is the second creator of the world who alone has given to the world its objective existence – without which, unheard, unseen, silently eating, giving birth, dying, heads nodding through hundreds of millions of years, it would have gone on in the profoundest night of non-being down to its unknown end.

**Carl Jung (1875–1961),
Swiss psychiatrist**

Individuals must discover the meaning of life for themselves. Those whose lives are most meaningful are those who don't need to ask, "Why are we here?" Of course, a stiff drink once in a while is not to be despised.

Peter Gay (b. 1923), US historian

There is no value on life except what you choose
to place upon it and no happiness in any place
except what you bring to it yourself.

Henry David Thoreau (1817–62), US writer

Life has meaning only if one
barters it day by day for something
other than itself.

Antoine de Saint-Exupery (1900–44), French novelist

Every man's life ends in the same way.
It is only the details of how he lived and how he died
that distinguish one man from another.

Ernest Hemingway (1899–1961), US novelist

Life consists not in holding good cards but in playing those you hold well.

Josh Billings (1818–85), US comedian

To live is to choose.
But to choose well, you must know
who you are and what you stand for,
where you want to go and why
you want to get there.

Kofi Annan (b. 1938), Ghanaian secretary-general of the United Nations

The purpose of life is a life of purpose.

Robert Byrne (b. 1928), US chess champion

Because man's quest for security is unending,
everyone can find meaning in life even if he dismisses
the question of the meaning of life as meaningless.

Sidney Hook (1902–89), US philosopher

There is no meaning to life except the meaning
man gives his life by the unfolding of his powers,
by living productively.

Erich Fromm (1900–80), German psychiatrist

To say that [existence] is ambiguous is to assert that meaning is never fixed, that it must constantly be won.

Simone de Beauvoir (1908–86), French writer and feminist

There are those who think that life is valueless because it comes to an end. They fail to see that the opposite argument might also be proposed: that if there were no end to life, life would have no value, that it is, in part, the ever-present danger of losing it which helps to bring home to us the value of life.

Karl Popper (1902–94), Austrian philosopher

Instead of looking at life as a narrow funnel,
we can see it ever widening to choose the things we
want to do, to take the wisdoms we've learned and
create something.

Liz Carpenter (b. 1920), US political campaigner

*All life is an experiment.
The more experiments you make,
the better.*

Ralph Waldo Emersor (1803–82), US philosopher

The hard truth seems to be this: we live in a vast and awesome universe in which, daily, suns are made and worlds destroyed, where humanity clings to an obscure clod of rock. The significance of our lives and our fragile realm derived from our own wisdom and courage. We are the custodians of life's meaning. We would prefer it to be otherwise, of course, but there is no compelling evidence for a cosmic Parent who will care for us and save us from ourselves. It is up to us.

Carl Sagan (1934–96), US astronomer

There is not one big cosmic meaning for all, there is only the meaning we each give to our life, an individual meaning, and individual plot, like an individual novel, a book for each person.

Anaïs Nin (1903–77), French-born US writer

The way to recover the meaning of life and the worthwhileness of life is to recover the power of experience, to have impulse voices from within, and to be able to hear these impulse voices from within – and make the point: this can be done.

Abraham Maslow (1908–70), US philosopher

Our obligation is to give meaning to life and in doing so, to overcome the passive, indifferent life.

Elie Wiesel (b. 1928), Romanian-born US writer

Love life above everything in the world ... love it, regardless of logic as you say, it must be regardless of logic, and it's only then one will understand the meaning of it.

Fyodor Dostoevsky (1821–81), Russian novelist

Man can will nothing unless he has first understood that he must count on no one but himself; that he is alone, abandoned on earth in the midst of his infinite responsibilities, without help, with no other aim than the one he sets himself, with no other destiny than the one he forges for himself on this earth.

Jean-Paul Sartre (1905–80), French writer and philosopher

We can gain comfort by believing in divine guidance, but in matters of the greatest importance we will be more prudent to depend on all the material knowledge and wisdom that humanity can summon up.

Edward Wilson (b. 1929), US biologist

*Life is what we make it,
always has been, always will be.*

Grandma Moses (1860–1961), US artist

Chapter 10

66 **Life is**

Life is something to do when you can't get to sleep.

Fran Lebowitz (b. 1951), US journalist

The absurd is the
essential concept
and the first truth.

Albert Camus (1913–60),
French writer

Life is a pantomime.

Bob Dylan (b. 1941), US singer-songwriter

Life is a joke that's just begun.

William Gilbert (1836–1911), English playwright and librettist

What is our life? A play of passion, our mirth the music of division, our mother's wombs the tiring house be where we dressed up for the short comedy.

Sir Walter Raleigh (1552–1618), English explorer

Isn't it the moment of most profound doubt
that gives birth to new certainties? Perhaps hopelessness
is the very soil that nourishes human hope; perhaps
one could never find sense in life without first
experiencing its absurdity.

Vaclav Havel (b. 1936), Czech playwright and politician

Does it not look as if existence were an error
the consequences of which gradually grow more
and more manifest.

Arthur Schopenhauer (1788–1860), German philosopher

Not a shred of evidence exists in favor of the idea that life is serious.

Brendan Gill (1914–1997), US critic

When we remember we are all mad, the mysteries disappear and life stands explained.

Mark Twain (1835–1910), US author

*Life is far too important a thing
to ever talk seriously about.*

Oscar Wilde (1854–1900), Irish writer

Stop worrying –
no one gets out of
this world alive!

Clive James (b. 1939), Australian writer and critic

Acknowledgements

Quotations

Among the many books and articles consulted for this collection, the editors wish to acknowledge the following publications:

Autobiography of Bertrand Russell, The (B. Russell, 1967); *Beautiful Boy* (J. Lennon, 1980); *Being and Nothingness* (J. P. Sartre, 1956); *Brief History of Time: A Reader's Companion* (S. Hawking, 1992); *Brothers Karamosov, The* (F. Dostoevsky); *Diary of Soren Kierkegaard, The* (S. Kierkegaard, 1843); *Doctor and the Soul, The* (V. Frankl, 1965); *Ethics of Ambiguity, The* (B. Frechtman, 1948); *Existential Psychotherapy* (I. Yalom, 1980); *Familiar Quotations* (J. Bartlett, 1968); *Freedom for Ministry* (R. J. Neuhaus, 1956); *Gales Quotations; Guardian, The* (28 December, 1977); *Healthy Personality, The: Readings* (H. Chiang and A. H. Maslow, 1969); *I and Thou* (M. Buber, 1958); *If You Meet the Buddha on the Road, Kill Him!* (S. B. Kopp); *Is Life Worth Living?* (C. Darrow); *John Stuart Mill: A Selection of His Works* (J. M. Robson, 1966); *Journey, The* (L. Smith, 1954); *Kitchen Table Wisdom* (N. R. Remen, 1996); *Last Word, The: A Treasury of Women's Quotes* (C. Warner, 1992); *Life and Work of Sigmund Freud, The* (E. Jones, 1953–57); *Little Minister, The* (J. M. Barrie); *Macbeth* (W. Shakespeare); *Malcolm X* (A. Haley); *Man for Himself* (E. Fromm, 1947); *Meaning in Life: the Creation of Value* (I. Singer, 1992); *Meaning of Life, The* (Friend et al., *Life* magazine, 1991); *Meaning of Life, The* (S. Sanders and D. R. Cheney); *Memories, Dreams, Reflections* (C. Jung, 1961); *Mikado, The* (W. Gilbert); *New York Times* (21 January, 1965); *Notebooks* (S. Butler, 1912); *Notebooks 1914–1916* (L. Wittgenstein, 1979); *On the Meaning of Life* (W. Durant, 1932); *Oxford Dictionary of Quotations, The* (1996); *Pale Fire* (V. Nabokov, 1962); *Pragmatism and the Tragic Sense of Life* (S. Hook, 1974); *Profiles in Courage* (J. F. Kennedy, 1948); *Quotable Woman, The: 1800–1975* (E. Partnow, 1977); *Sacred Hoops* (P. Jackson); *Search for the Truth* (M. Herrick, 1968); *Seinlanguage* (J. Seinfeld); *Simple Wisdom* (G. Jones, 1997); *Simpson's Contemporary Quotations* (J. B. Simpson, 1988); *Story of My Life, The* (C. Darrow); *Tempest, The* (W. Shakespeare); *The Routledge Dictionary of Quotations* (R. Andrews, 1987); *Tractatus logico-philosophicus* (L. Wittgenstein, 1961); *Webster's New World Dictionary of Quotable Definitions; What Mad Pursuit* (F. Crick, 1988); *What's Good* (L. Reed, 1992); *Will to Meaning, The* (V. Frankl, 1969); *Wisdom of the Heart, The* (H. Miller, 1947).

Picture Credits

All photographs courtesy of Getty Images except: p. 23 ™ 2004 James Dean by CMG Worldwide, Inc. www.jamesdean.com
p. 150 Courtesy of The Albert Einstein Archives, The Hebrew University of Jerusalem

I believe that the very purpose of our life is to seek happiness. That is clear. Whether one believes in religion or not, whether one believes in this religion or that religion, we are all seeking something better in life. So, I think, the very motion of our lives is towards happiness.

The Dalai Lama (b. 1935), Tibetan religious leader